HIERONYMUS BOSCH

ABOUT THE AUTHOR

Anthony Bosman, distinguished Dutch art critic,
is the general editor of this series.

ANTHONY BOSMAN

Hieronymus Bosch

BARNES & NOBLE, INC.

NEW YORK

Publishers • Booksellers • Since 1873

Editor: Anthony Bosman
Translation: Albert J. Fransella
Lay-out: Wim van Stek
Published in the United States in 1963
by Barnes & Noble, Inc., 105 Fifth Avenue, New York 3, N.Y.
© 1962 and printed in Holland by The Ysel Press Ltd, Deventer
Second printing, 1967

HIERONYMUS BOSCH

Few painters of the late Middle Ages so enthral and intrigue us as does Hieronymus Bosch; indeed, in our century his works are meeting with a very wide response. For they enable us to conjure up the life of a period characterized—as is our own—by a sense of spiritual uncertainty, a breaking away from established standards of behaviour, which were being hypocritically maintained in principle but at the same time deliberately ignored and violated in practice.

In its double function of maintaining the old artistic forms of painting and of introducing a new spirit difficult to explain, the work of Bosch—set between the Middle Ages and the Renaissance—is extremely typical of a period of transition, a time of revolutionary change, in which old beliefs are being assailed, while new ones are not yet recognized or acknowledged. Out of all this emerges the image of a life dominated by the anxiety of the individual, and it was in the days of Hieronymus Bosch, towards the end of the fifteenth and the beginning of the sixteenth centuries, that this anxiety began to reveal itself. It emanated from the new direction religious thought was taking, from man's recent conquest of an earthly reality, which resulted in an urge to become free of all-embracing hierarchical impositions. In those days of spiritual transition, these factors gave the individual a feeling of inner uncertainty which expressed itself in widely differing ways.

We have indeed come to realize, since the publication in 1919 of Professor Huizinga's book *The Waning of the Middle Ages,* that in actual fact the spirit of the fifteenth century was very much the reverse of that seemingly reflected by the pictorial arts. In every respect it was a century of extravagance; life itself was fierce and passionate. We have only to turn to the chronicles of those times to read descriptions of luxurious and often quite absurd pomp, of political ambitions carried to the wildest extremes, totally regardless of all consequences.

How can we reconcile the deep religious sense, the serenity, of the pictorial arts with the boundless ostentation of the festivities in which the nobility sought distraction from the oppression of the time? Search for a solution as we may, debauchery and religious sense cannot be reconciled, unless we decide to accept an enigmatic fusion of two heterogeneous elements such as religion and worldliness. It would appear from the chronicles of those days that such a synthesis was possible; devout prayer used to follow sensual festivities, while cupidity went hand in hand with piety, and pride with modesty. It seems that all limits had become obscured, as though all human virtues and vices could be blended together, perhaps inextricably so.

Doubt and uncertainty, anxiety and fear, sought other outlets than worldly merrymaking; they tried to find them in a piety which bore the same marks of extravagance. War and pestilence raged throughout the Netherlands during the whole of the fifteenth century, famine and poverty ravaged the populace, injustice and violence reigned everywhere. Processions passed in endless columns through the countryside, chanting and scourging themselves, almost neurotically testifying to the sinfulness of man. These manifestations were coupled with meetings led by preachers urging repentance, men who knew how to whip the masses to a religious frenzy far surpassing normal emotion. Religion itself also went through a crisis which resulted in the formation of many sects and eventually led to the Reformation. The silent religious inner convictions of the early Middle Ages had given place to a boisterousness and an outward behaviour which betrayed all too well the anxiety of mind to which the people had fallen prey.

No other painter has presented this side of life as vividly as Hieronymus Bosch has. For a long time he was looked upon as just a "maker of devils," a curiosity, whose paintings were amusing and sometimes very grisly inventions, worth admiring because of the ingenuity he showed in portraying the denizens of Hell. He was regarded as a figure not properly belonging to his time, an individualist whose painting was dominated by a bizarre, sometimes even a morbid, imagination.

But the work of an artist cannot be considered in isolation. One cannot solve the mysteries of form and content by immersing oneself in the details of the work. It is essential to see the threads which run from the work via the human being to the structure of the times.

In our own century it has become clearer than ever that the artist is not an autonomous power. For concentrated in him are the forces of the life of his period, of its spirit and of its actuality, all of which, filtered through his personality, can give utterance—positive or negative—to what lives in man and in human nature. For a long time the artist has been regarded either as a kind of reproductive creature, registering like a seismograph the vibrations of life, or purely as a personality creating out of the solitude of his own psychic nature. He is neither the one nor the other. Rather should he be seen as one who—through the medium of his art—lays bare the life of his times and interprets it in shapes and forms.

But before we can proceed from here with Bosch, we are halted by almost insuperable difficulties. Separated from him by less than five centuries, we can understand the religious thought, the literature, the sociological structure, and the life of his times, but all the same he himself remains a riddle to us, now that we no longer see in him the "maker of devils" but try to elucidate the essence of his art.

That holds, at any rate, for a portion of his work, the altarpieces in which he portrays Heaven and Hell: "The Hay Wagon" and "The Garden of Earthly Delights" in the Prado in Madrid, and "The Temptation of St. Anthony" in the Museum in Lisbon (pp. 26-32, 56-65, 38-45).

The problem which now immediately presents itself—and which goes much farther than the question of how Bosch came to conceive his diableries—is that of the actual sense of these works and their extremely enigmatic meaning. Generally speaking, it has been assumed that they served to remind the simple churchgoer of the rudiments of his faith, for religious emotion was the only readily understandable language in the Middle Ages, even in the latter part, in the time of Bosch. The spirit of a work of art was that of the Creed itself. Always we see paintings of heavenly raptures and menaces, representing a life full of piety and the fear of God. Where a place in the heavenly order was vouchsafed to anything mundane, then this earthly thing was merely a reflection of the reality in Heaven. The function of the work of art was to act as a continuous reminder of the Divine greatness and of the elements of the Creed.

Therefore art—which was always ecclesiastical art—had to speak in a language understood by everybody, a language as current as the letters of the alphabet. Just as this had been laid down and every character had its own meaning, so was every form an iconographically determined symbol. A strict convention was imposed upon the artist: every picture had its iconographic code for its symbolic content. Even the colour was prescribed. Art in the Middle Ages was pre-eminently a communal art because it derived its make-up from the dominating belief and because its mission was to glorify the foundation upon which the community was built: the Christian faith.

These assumptions have become the basis for efforts to unravel the enigma of Hieronymus Bosch. With the aid of Biblical writings and the literature of his day, proverbs, folklore, and even astrology, it has been possible to arrive at explanations of much of what is depicted in the great altarpieces. Each interpretation has only a theoretical value and is attacked again and again by those who think they have discovered a more revealing key to Bosch. For his contemporaries his symbolic delineations may well have been quite obvious; for us in the twentieth century his fantasies are to a great extent incomprehensible, and we can only guess at their meaning.

But even if his altarpieces could be explained scene by scene —and there are hundreds of these—there still remains the much more interesting riddle of the painter Hieronymus Bosch himself as the creator of an obsessive world, inspired by a fantasy which is really incredible, and for which one cannot find the like in his time.

Incidentally, many points of contact are discernible. The grotesque fantasy of the Middle Ages flourished in the sculpture of the Romanesque and Gothic cathedrals. There, on their capitals, their flying buttresses, and their roof gutters, dwell the monsters of Hell. These satanic figures, stretching out their claws towards man, are personified with a visionary strength. There in the Romanesque period this apocalyptic world took shape, horrible and abominable. The Gothic devils, generally

Self-portrait of Hieronymus Bosch
Drawing in the Codex of Atrecht

speaking, are not quite as grim; they are gruesome in an amusing kind of way, possessing as a rule a certain quality of caricature, which in late Gothic even tends to become comical.

Hieronymus Bosch could have found models in that sculpture, and also in the breviaries, in the choir-stalls, and of course in the apocalyptic literature and the fantasies of the rhetoricians, who, as Kalff described in his *History of the Literature of the Netherlands*, "caused a wooden spade to bound along on iron clogs, a broomstick to walk with a limp, and a mortar to have a headache" (*vide* Brom, *Painting and Literature in the 16th and 17th Centuries*).

There is, however, a great gulf between the devils on the cathedrals and those created by Bosch. The devils of stone and on paper always remained subservient to the imaginative world of man; after all, they were "human devils" in spite of their satanic frightfulness. Emile Mâle once wrote: "The demon of the thirteenth century is no monster; he is merely a man depraved by vice . . ."

The devilish monsters of Bosch are entirely different phenomena. They no longer have anything in common with humanity, but are terrifying pieces of machinery, put together out of the elements of man, animal, and thing, ghastly creatures to whom the painter has given a fantastic life. And they are all the more horrible because they originate from sharp observation. Nothing is hidden; each part out of which they are formed is an actual element. Their demonic character arises out of the union of the existing world with the realm of dreams.

No wonder, then, that in our own times the surrealists have appropriated Bosch as a most eminent predecessor, who, five hundred years earlier than they, gave form to the infernal workings of the human soul in torment. The dream world was the domain of the surrealists and hellish were their conceptions, which defied any reasonable interpretation and could only be approached by way of the doctrines of Freud and the interpretation of the unconscious, based in many cases upon the effect of shock. Consciously, the relation between the image and reality became more remote until, in the end, the image acquired an independent existence of its own, and with it the value of a psychographic revelation.

Undoubtedly something of all this is also to be traced in Bosch himself. It is just not possible to explain his extremely personal monsters as being derived from the literature or from any other expression of his time. The fiendish figures must have come out of *him*, for only too often there is a sort of chuckling satisfaction in his work, in the manner in which he causes his fantastic spectres to torment humanity. No earthly martyrdom seems to satisfy him. Always he is inventing new devilish shapes, which in refined and sometimes perverse fashion make man atone for his sinful life on earth. The whole gamut of his powers of imagination in this respect is unlimited, and all the cruelties that human beings are capable of inflicting upon one another are child's play compared with what Hieronymus Bosch permits the damned to suffer.

What kind of a man was Bosch? The facts of his life give no answer; in truth, we know nothing of the actual man. What we have been able to gather from archives gives us no decisive answer. He must have been born about 1450 in 's-Hertogen-bosch as Jheronimus van Aken (or Aeken), and came of a family that had already been known for many years in Den Bosch as painters. The name Van Aken appeared for the first time in the archives of the year 1399, in which a certain Jan van Aken was mentioned as a furrier by trade who had acquired the freedom of the city. This Jan van Aken, perhaps a forebear of Hieronymus, might well have come from Aachen, as his name suggests, for traces of the family lead to that city. This Jan van Aken died in 1418.

Though we are pretty vague about the relationship between the furrier and Hieronymus Bosch, we are able to be quite definite about the next Jan van Aken, who from 1423 to 1434 was repeatedly mentioned in the records of the St. Jan's Church in Den Bosch, and who, in the years 1435 and 1436, is referred to as a painter. This man was the grandfather of Hieronymus Bosch. The father of Hieronymus was Antonius van Aken, a painter, who lived from about 1416 to 1478. In 1477 Hieronymus Bosch married Aleid van de Meervenne, of patrician parents, and it is on the basis of this date that his estimated year of birth was accepted as 1450. Three years after his marriage we find Bosch mentioned for the first time in the registers of the

Brotherhood of Our Lady as "Jeroen die Maelre" (Jerome the Painter). In 1486 he became a member of the Brotherhood, and after that his name appeared regularly in the registers for 1488 (when he was promoted to Notable or Sworn Brother), 1493-94, 1498-99, 1508-9, and 1512. In 1516 the same registers contained the record of his decease: "*Obitus fratrum: Ao 1516 Hieronimus Aquen alias Bosch insignis pictor* (famous painter)."

It was the end of what was considered in those days a long life. Of actual facts we know nothing more. As a person, Hieronymus Bosch remains a mystery. From his marriage with Aleid van de Meervenne, through whom, in 1484, he came into possession of the country estate of Rodeke near Oirschot, we may deduce that he was not just an ordinary painter but, thanks to the property of his wife, also a man of standing. And from the addition of the words "famous painter" in the registration of his death we can infer that during his own lifetime he was already a celebrated artist—in the first place, of course, in Den Bosch, where he worked and lived.

When Alart Duhameel, the architect of the important extension and completion of St. Jan's Church in the years 1478 to 1494, designed a new chapel for the Brotherhood of Our Lady, it was Hieronymus Bosch who, in 1494-95, made the designs for the stained-glass windows. Moreover, he executed for St. Jan's six paintings: "The Creation of the World," "Abigail with Solomon," "The Adoration of the Magi," "The Siege of Bethulia, with the Murder of Holophernes," "The Flight of the Army after the Murder," and "Esther before Ahasuerus." As late as 1611 these works were still being described, but in 1629, after the capture of Den Bosch, the Catholic clergy, with the permission of Prince Frederik Hendrik, took away the paintings, and they disappeared without a trace.

The renown of Hieronymus Bosch had, however, spread far beyond the provincial art centre of 's-Hertogenbosch. Philip the Handsome, Duke of Burgundy and Archduke of Austria, commissioned him to paint a large picture of "The Last Judgment" in 1504, and in September of that year sent him an advance with the following note: "To Jeronimus van Aeken, called Bosch, painter, living at 's-Hertogenbosch, the sum of XXXVI pounds as advance on what he will be owed for a

12

large painting nine feet high and nine feet long, which is to be the Last Judgment, with Paradise and Hell, which the Monseigneur has commissioned him to execute to the satisfaction of His Highness."

It is evident, from inventories, that the Stadholder Margaret of Austria possessed (in 1516) a "Temptation of St. Anthony" by Bosch; that Cardinal Grimani had in his collection a "Hell" by Bosch; and that the painting "The Cure of Folly" (p. 19), which is now in the Prado in Madrid, was in 1524 in the possession of Bishop Philip of Burgundy at Duurstede Castle near Utrecht. Finally the art connoisseur Felipe de Guevara, a confidant of the Emperor Charles V, took back several works to Spain, where later on they came into the possession of Philip II, the ascetic, suspicious king who had tried to exterminate the Reformation in the Netherlands by fire and sword. Having withdrawn from the outside world to his palace, the present Escorial, the king consoled himself with the works of Hieronymus Bosch, examples of the art the king loved best. According to witnesses, the painting "The Seven Deadly Sins" (pp. 20, 21) was the last thing the king saw; it hung opposite his deathbed in the little cell where he passed through his death agony.

That, then, is the picture of the painter, gathered from the archives. It tells us something of the respect and renown which he enjoyed, and of the dissemination of his art, but it leaves unsolved the riddle of the man himself.

There exists a portrait of Bosch, a drawing in the Codex of Atrecht, which portrays the painter probably in the last years of his life (p. 9). He wears the clothes of a simple man, his face is gaunt and wrinkled, the neck—like that of a plucked bird—reveals the taut muscles which support the head. The mouth is remarkable, almost a straight line, with only a trace of lips. Then the massive nose, and the chin which emphasizes the resoluteness of the face. The eyes, however, are the most fascinating feature, seeming to lead a private life of their own. They have not grown old, like the rest of the face, but are keen and alert, dominating and even aggressive.

There we have the man behind the paintings, behind those hellish fantasies of the imagination, the effect of which even in our century has not grown weaker. We have tried to rediscover

13

him in his paintings, for an artist who, on the one hand, gives free rein to a grotesque fantasy, and, on the other hand, shows himself to be a keen-eyed realist, could hardly refrain from putting something of himself into his pictures. Marcel Brion thought he had found Hieronymus Bosch in a creature possessing only a head and a pair of legs, who is sitting opposite St. Anthony in the central panel of the Lisbon "Temptation" (p. 41); again in the right-hand wing of "The Garden of Earthly Delights" as a monster contrived out of an eggshell and the branches of a tree stripped of their bark, which carries on the head it is turning towards the onlooker a circular board with a bagpipe (p. 61); and finally in the second figure from the left of "The Crowning with Thorns" (p. 66).

In this last painting the man with the curly hair, the massive nose, the bent chin jutting forward, and the eyes gazing sympathetically is the only recognizable portrait; the other figures, the judge and the executioners, have deliberately exaggerated expressions on their faces. They are clearly just types; not so the man looking on. Indeed, there is a very definite likeness between the man in "The Crowning with Thorns" and the Atrecht portrait, but the difference in age is too great to permit one to determine the similarity with certainty. The same may be said for the two other presumed self-portraits, although a resemblance can be seen which to some extent justifies Brion's assumption.

Again, two self-portraits have been discovered, one in the foremost figure of the three men in the left wing of "The Temptation of St. Anthony" who are bringing the saint over the little bridge to his cave (p. 40), and the other in the face of "The Vagabond," formerly called "The Prodigal Son" (p. 71). None of the other supposed self-portraits comes as close to the portrait in the Codex of Atrecht as do these two.

The puzzle is interesting, but defies solution. Hieronymus Bosch as a person can only be approached through his work and the times in which it appeared.

In our day we have a new device, certainly not very beatific, but extremely revealing: psychoanalysis. Clinically and analytically this fifteenth-century man called Bosch has been plucked out of his work, without taking into account the

14

times in which he lived. No psychiatrist has ever had a more perplexing case brought to his consulting room. Everything in the way of erotic or sexual deviation might be attributed to this painter Bosch. He is an invert, an anal erotic, a sadist, a fetichist of the worst kind, he suffers from both infantile and senile sexual perversities, he is a masochist, a phallus-worshipper —in short, Hieronymus Bosch is a hellish bundle of all the psychic illnesses that Freud and Jung have discovered. There is too much of it for it to be credible. Rather than concede that Bosch had such an impossibly perverted personality (though we readily grant him an isolated aberration), we are forced to believe in a Freud before his time, in an acute observer of life around him, which he depicted with humour but without mercy.

However, we must not forget that Bosch—and this makes him the complete opposite to twentieth-century surrealists—painted Hell and holiness side by side, not with one complementing the other, but always with the saintly in struggle against the infernal, the satanic. It is true that the saintly beings always occupy but a small portion of his painting, an insignificant one compared with the hordes of devilish creatures, but St. Anthony, St. John, St. Jerome are there, unyieldingly resisting the temptations and the terrors to which they are subjected, inviolable no matter what sort of hellish beings are loosed upon them. The saints of Bosch may be tempted as never before, and with means never thought of by any other human mind, but they resist and justify their holy state, which is ever the beginning and the end.

For that matter, Bosch did not paint only diableries, though that part of his work is the most fascinating. Time and time again he shows himself as a good, devout man of the Middle Ages, who does not deviate from the conventional ideas.

This is evident from his early pictures of "The Bearing of the Cross" and those such as "St. Christopher" (p. 36), "St. John at Patmos" (p. 55), and "The Adoration of the Magi" (p. 69). In these works the artist is the typical man of the fifteenth century who is aware that he is tied to a certain system of symbols, and settles everything in obedient relationship towards the Divine. He may be forgiven for not being able to refrain from inserting a few strange creatures and objects into some of his works.

15

The pitcher hanging in a tree, to which ladders give entry, in the painting of "St. Christopher" (p. 36), the little imp behind St. John at Patmos (p. 55), and the odd little man on the roof of the stable at Bethlehem in "The Adoration of the Magi" (p. 69) are of scarcely any importance, merely additions by a mind that cannot desist from a little "devilry." They play no essential part in the action or setting of the pictures; in fact, their function is the same as that of the diabolical figures in stone on the cathedrals, in which the Gothic sculptors indulged their whimsical and roguish fantasies.

Hieronymus Bosch is, however, more firmly bound to the early fifteenth century by his compositional structure and artist's style than by the iconographically prescribed scene. In certain respects these do not correspond with the regenerative tendencies which are to be observed in the work of his contemporaries. Bosch did not bother himself with a logical perspective, his compositions are flat, there is no spatial cohesion between the figures and the background, and the horizon is always set very high.

Two factors can explain this traditional setting: firstly, the connection that exists between Bosch's style and the art of the miniature and, secondly, his need for as large a foreground as possible into which a multitude of figures and scenes can be placed. This result he could only achieve by keeping his compositions as flat as possible and giving them very little depth.

These are all characteristics of an illustrative artist, of which the source can be found in the miniatures with which chiefly breviaries, but also Bibles, missals, and prayerbooks were illuminated. The word "miniature" in this connection does not imply smallness of dimensions. It is derived from *minium*, or *menie*, the red paint with which capital letters used to be drawn in the early Middle Ages. From the decoratively designed letter there developed an illustration containing human beings and animals, which kept on taking up more room and finally spread over a whole page. Then the gamut of colours became larger; the bright blue of lapis lazuli, yellow, white ground colour, incarnadine (flesh colour), gold, and mixed colours (such as violet and green) were all added to the minium. The miniature became a gem of the painter's art, but did not belie its illustrative and decorative character, not even when, in the beginning of the fifteenth century, the miniature came under the influence of the art of panel painting, and the background of gold leaf made way for landscapes and interiors.

The simple calligraphic initial developed with the miniature. It became the playground of the miniaturist, in which he was able to indulge his fondness for parti-coloured forms, which he extended to the margins, so that the whole page became a luxurious feast of colour, decoration, and imagery. It was particularly in the margins that he was able to give rein to his imagination and to permit the existence of the incompatible. That is where the queer beings, the infernal creatures, are to be found, as for instance in the Utrecht Breviary of Yolande de Lalaing, in the Bodleian Library at Oxford.

The bonds between Hieronymus Bosch and the art of miniatures in his century are threefold: there are the similarities in composition; the miniature had been one of his sources of inspiration for his world of fantastic creatures; and he became linked up with the genre and the morality painters miniaturists had become.

His earliest works are directly connected with the art of the miniature, both spiritually and in structure. In contrast with his contemporaries he proceeded much further with the genre picture, and gave this such an individual life that he may well be described as the first Netherlands genre painter. His very earliest works, "The Cure of Folly" (p. 19), the scenes of "The Seven Deadly Sins"—of which "Anger" (p. 20) and "Gluttony" (p. 21) are illustrated—and "The Conjurer" (p. 25) are splendid examples of genre.

"The Cure of Folly" (p. 19) even retains the shape of the miniature. Its circular form, the enclosing of the picture in a frame filled in with calligraphic ornamentation, and the inscription: "Master, cut the stone out quickly—My name is Lubbert Das," all this tallies exactly with the miniature. Hieronymus Bosch, however, goes further than any miniaturist. He is not merely illustrating, he is reproducing a keenly observed actuality, which he interprets in his own burlesque, and grotesque, manner.

He has decked out the "Medicine Master" with a funnel on his head, symbol of the charlatan, who has convinced the anxious-looking wretch in the chair that he will cure him of his folly by cutting the stone out of his skull, as medieval superstition would have it. A monk with a tankard in his hand is encouraging the patient, and an old woman leaning on a table is looking on, with the book of knowledge upon her head.

This genre piece is perfect, but Bosch would not have belonged to the Middle Ages if he had not introduced a moralizing meaning to justify the painting. The quack represents evil, to which man yields in his stupidity. Even the Church is deceived by it. If it is true, as some think, that the old woman is a nun and the book on her head is the Bible, then this little genre painting assumes the character of an attack upon the clergy, who allow themselves to be blinded by the sorcerer's arts of a heretical demon, who is indicated as such by the pitcher—the sign of Satan—at his girdle.

The painting "The Seven Deadly Sins" (pp. 20, 21), which is a table-top and so must be viewed from above, shows Bosch to a still greater extent as a painter of the life of the people, a forerunner of Pieter Brueghel the Elder—who was greatly influenced by Bosch—and of Jan Steen. These paintings are no allegories, but striking little scenes from everyday life by which he illustrates the deadly sins, although here too symbolism is by no means absent.

In the four corners of the painting we see, illustrated in medallions, Death (a dying man being comforted by clergy), the Last Judgment, Hell, and Paradise. They are small scenes, which very clearly originate from the miniature, not only iconographically and as regards composition, but also spiritually. Bosch had learned nothing, or had not wished to learn anything, from the school of Jan van Eyck; the persons are poorly modelled, they are even rendered with a certain clumsiness.

All the same, they herald the first typical elements of the work of Bosch—naturally, we are almost moved to say, in Hell. There Hell burns in the background; rather in the sense of the words of Carel van Mander, who lived a century after Bosch, and who said of him: "How pleasant and natural he was with flames and burning, and fire and smoke," than of actual cities

18

(Continued on page 73)

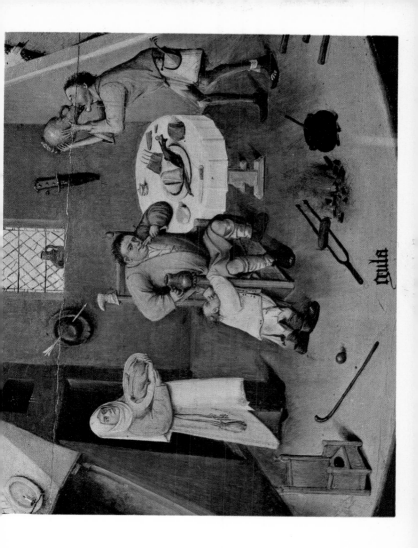

22

34

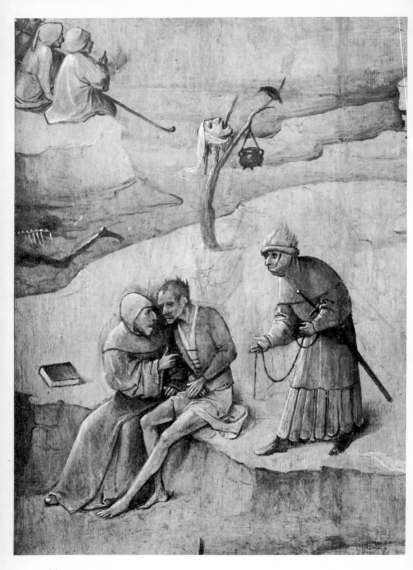

45

48

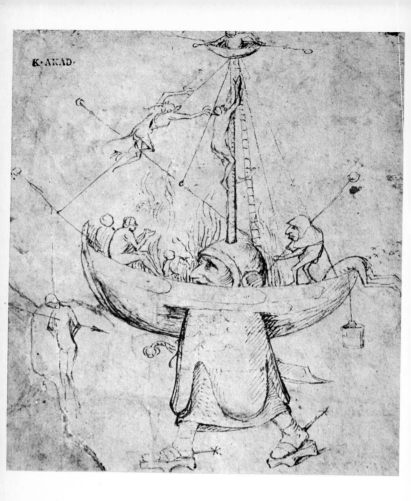

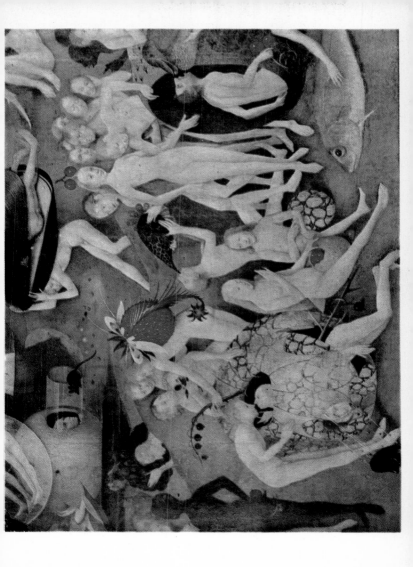

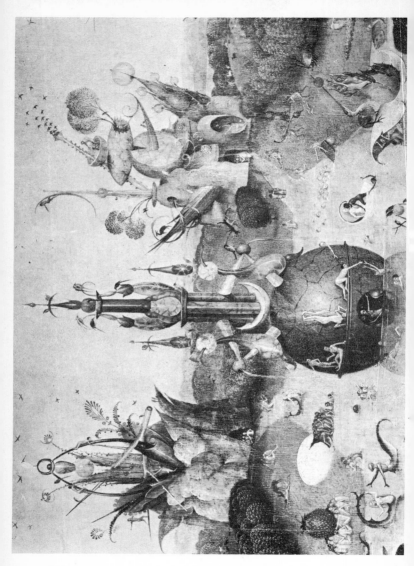

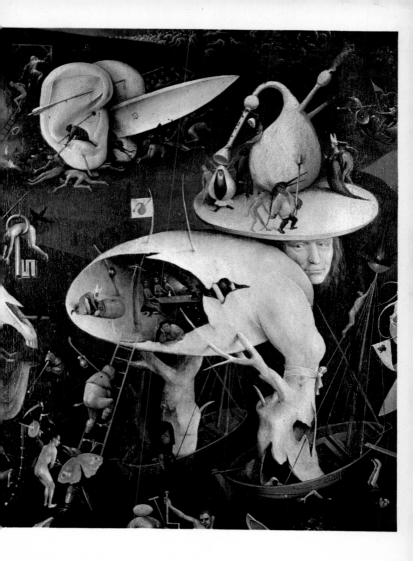

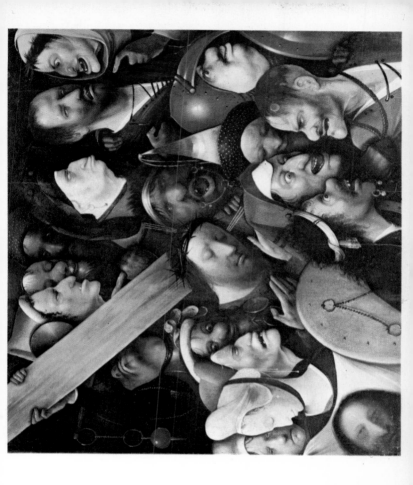

69

71

burning, which we see later in the pictures of Hell itself (p. 60). In the inferno of the "Seven Deadly Sins" we also meet with the first monsters, but they are still just traditional devils, not the hellish machines a thousand times more frightening which, later on, Bosch was to put together with such tremendous ingenuity.

In the centre of the painting, in a circular composition divided into seven segments, the Seven Deadly Sins are illustrated, and in the middle Christ is seen rising from the grave, and uttering the warning: *"Cave, Cave, Deus videt"* (Beware, Beware; God sees). "Anger" (p. 20), "Vanity," "Lust," "Sloth," "Gluttony" (p. 21), "Covetousness," and "Envy" are all presented here in quite good-natured little scenes, which have none of the fierceness which Bosch renders in his later paintings of the sins of man. They are moral pictures, rather more amusing than frightening, and the sins, by no means great, are eminently human.

Anger is a fight between drunken men; Vanity, a woman before whom a little demon is holding a mirror; Lust, a convivial gathering of a few couples; Gluttony, a household à la Jan Steen, where people are greedily consuming pigs' trotters, ham, ribs of beef, sausage, and roast goose.

In the same strain as "The Cure of Fools" is "The Conjurer" (p. 25), a painting moralizing in a humorous manner, which strikes us on the one hand by the realism which underlies it, and on the other hand by the somewhat caricaturing exaggeration, through which humour, almost entirely lacking in fifteenth-century art, becomes a precious attribute.

In front of a table stands a conjurer, whose tricks so fascinate one man among the sceptical onlookers that another man standing behind him makes use of the occasion to pilfer his purse. Obviously the conjurer is a demon. Just as with the quack in "The Cure of Folly," an attribute discloses this to us; here it is an owl which sticks its head out of the little wicker basket hanging from the girdle of the conjurer. In this way Bosch conveyed to his contemporaries the idea that illusions only make one poorer.

It is particularly difficult to place religious works such as "The Marriage at Cana" and "Ecce Homo" in the sphere of these genre paintings. "The Marriage at Cana" (p. 24) does, how-

73

ever, show the same genre-like approach to the subject. We can now perceive a phenomenon gradually taking place which was later on, in the sixteenth century, to occur pretty generally, namely, the gradual elimination of the strictly religious theme and the coming more and more to the fore of the still life and the landscape. Christ's miracle of changing the water into wine takes place almost unnoticed; it is only a small part of the whole of the action. No one seems to have noticed the miracle except the man sitting at Christ's left (possibly the patron of the artist).

This is not to be explained by the simultaneous representation of what in fact were consecutive occurrences—the noticing that there is no more wine, the changing of the water into wine, and the offering of the goblet of wine to the bridal couple. If we analyze the painting we come up against a quantity of symbols which indicate that Bosch wanted to make this work of far more significance than just "The Marriage at Cana." He sets the good (the miracle Jesus performed) against the evil, which is frequently present in the painting. The meat courses, which are being carried in on the left, consist of unclean animals—a fire-spitting swan and the head of a pig; in the background a sorcerer is standing at a kind of altar. These elements could point to heresy; according to Bax, to the Semitic heretics who practised a secret worship of Egyptian or Syrian origin.

Whatever interpretation is given to this picture, it has undeniably a dualistic character which—as will become evident—constantly occurs with Bosch, and has given rise to hypotheses about the religious beliefs of the painter.

In "Ecce Homo" (pp. 22, 23), we find again the Hieronymus Bosch of the genre paintings, for this exhibiting of Christ to the mob must surely be called a genre piece, taken from passion plays or suchlike, because in its essence this picture is "theatre". We see a pitiable Christ, whose body is covered with wounds (originally a garment had been painted over it); behind him is Pontius Pilate, and around him the executioners. It was not, however, to this portion of the picture that Bosch had given fullest emphasis—the faces are flat and lack personality—but to the rabble below, who cry "Crucify him!" and bear witness to their hate for him in their venomous, distorted, and sneering countenances. We should say their "devilish" hate, for in symbols Bosch makes it plain that the Devil is controlling these people, and we may even conjecture that the artist took the theme of heresy from his "Marriage at Cana."

After "Ecce Homo" we come to the first great work (of those still in existence): the triptych "The Hay Wagon" (pp. 26–32), the first of an impressive series, which must have been begun between 1485 and 1490 and have continued into the first decade of the next century. This series includes "The Hay Wagon," "The Temptation of St. Anthony," and "The Garden of Earthly Delights," three works in which Hieronymus Bosch attained an originality which one can try to approach but can never satisfactorily interpret. It is as though his sardonic imagination suddenly breaks loose and knows no restraints in the creation of an endless stream of monsters, of hallucinations become flesh which swarm over his paintings — but hallucinations having their origins in actual sins, hellish caricatures of sharply observed realities.

With that outburst of the fantastic the artist's technique alters, becomes smoother, more natural, more facile. From "The Cure of Folly" up to and including "Ecce Homo" we see the painter developing. At first he is still completely tied to the miniature and to the earlier painting style of the fifteenth century. Moreover, technically he is not yet fully able to realize his purposes. There are broken folds in the costumes, which are not in keeping with the movements; there are faces and gestures which lack character of their own; the postures of the people are stiff (this is most striking in "The Marriage at Cana") and the bodies are awkwardly rendered. In short, all this indicates the provincial education of the artist, who dwelt outside the great art centres where he could have studied the problems of spatiality and natural modelling.

Over the years Bosch did develop; his drawing became freer, the folds of his costumes lost their unnaturalness and indicated movement, his undeveloped style acquired rich colouring, with a fine touch applied effectively and surely, while the modelling of the faces became more refined and more expressive. It was with these accomplishments that Bosch was

equipped when he commenced his triptych "The Hay Wagon."
He was master of his palette, of his brushwork, of his drawing,
and of his imagination.

One can seek in the past for a parallel case, but in vain. Nothing
can be found, either among the miniaturists or among the
popular prints, which could serve as an example. The audacity
of his imagination stamps him as a unique figure, as a man of
the new era, which spiritually leaves the Middle Ages far
behind and yet is closely bound up with it in other ways;
as an interpreter of the sentiments which ruled in a life only
recognizable to twentieth-century people in general terms.

The middle panel of "The Hay Wagon" (pp. 27, 29, 32) is an
astounding allegory based on Isaiah 40: 6-8 "All flesh is grass
[in older Bibles, hay] and all the goodliness thereof is as the
flower of the field: The grass withereth, the flower fadeth;
because the spirit of the Lord bloweth upon it: surely the people
is grass. The grass withereth, the flower fadeth: but the word
of our God shall stand for ever."

In addition, Bosch illustrated the proverb: "The world is a
haystack; everyone grabs what he can lay hands on," for the
panel shows a hay wagon upon which all and sundry, armed
with ladders and hay forks, throw themselves as though
possessed. Men and women, monks and nuns, jostle each
other round the wagon, grabbing, pushing each other and
fighting, falling and getting under the wheels (p. 32).

The hay wagon is being drawn along by monsters, half-
animal, half-human, who are bringing the people to Hell.
Behind the wagon comes a procession of the great ones of this
world, of princes and prelates, of emperor and pope in great
pomp. On top of the hay (p. 29) there are a couple of lovers
sitting down and another couple behind them standing up,
flanked by an angel praying and a devil playing music—a
charming image of sin, as gentle as in "The Seven Deadly
Sins." Above all this appears the figure of Christ, looking
down upon all these happenings with a gesture of despair.

The left panel, on which the creation of Eve, the temptation,
and the expulsion from Paradise are depicted (pp. 26, 30) is
much more traditional, with the exception of the falling angels
in the topmost portion, where the rebellious angels are depicted

as a swarm of vermin threatening to descend upon Paradise.

The right panel is a continuation of the procession in the central panel, which is marching straight into Hell (pp. 26, 31). The sinners are being waylaid by devils and driven to a tower still under construction, with a blazing ruin in the background.

This triptych is (like all the following ones) a piling up of scenes, each of which has its significance in the gamut of the Seven Deadly Sins. The brushwork of the painting is delicate, the colouring is transparent, and it reminds one of the words of Carel van Mander: "He [Bosch] had a firm and very proficient and pleasant action [technique], painting in many of his figures straightaway, which, without alteration, still remain very beautiful." The spontaneity of the brushwork is very striking, as it gives the painting a lightness of accent in spite of the multiplicity of events.

Finally, Bosch painted on the outside shutters of the side panels, not in a variety of colours but in grisaille, a wandering fool roving anxiously through the countryside, and in the background some robbers stripping a merchant to the skin, a couple of peasants dancing to the music of the bagpipes, and, in the distance, a gallows (p. 28). This painting is a forerunner of the famous picture "The Vagabond," which Bosch painted in his most mature period (pp. 70, 71). Artistically and spiritually closely akin to "The Hay Wagon" is "The Ship of Fools" (p. 33), in which one finds again the figures who are trying to seize the hay in the middle panel of "The Hay Wagon." Now, however, they are merrymakers in a small boat, manned by fools sailing to the paradise of madness.

This theme was familiar in the Middle Ages. There may be some connection with didactic literature such as *De Blauwe Schuit* (The Blue Boat) of Jacob van Oestvoren (1413), with its similar gathering of half-wits, and with the poem *Das Narrenschiff* (The Ship of Fools) by the humanist Sebastian Brant, which appeared in 1494 in an illustrated edition at Basle and was a satire upon the licentiousness of his time.

Hieronymus Bosch has painted the subject with popular humour and mordant realism, a realism, however, always permeated by the fantastic and the grotesque. The centre of attention is the lute-playing nun, who, with the monk sitting

77

opposite her, is singing what is certainly by no means a religious song, in which she is joined by the others, unless they are drinking or quarrelling. Drivel, lewdness, debauchery are depicted here, as indeed many symbols further indicate (such as the cherries on the table, the bundle of hazel branches, the jester, the owl, etc.).

It is an enchanting painting, not only in expressions and effective delineation of types, but also as far as composition is concerned in the contrast between the foolish company and the serene landscape, and artistically in the sparkling manner in which the paint has been applied.

Hell and Paradise, devils and saints, continue to occupy the imagination of the painter. It may be a praying St. Jerome, an emaciated penitent, who lies stretched out upon some rocky ground and is surrounded by a disturbing landscape strewn with symbols of alchemy and heresy (p. 35), which are in flagrant contradiction to the peaceful scene in the background (p. 34). Or it may be a Saint Christopher, who wades with the Holy Child through a river (p. 36), wearied because, according to the legend of the giant Reprobus, it would appear that in carrying the Christ Child on his back, he carries also the sins of the whole world. Bosch also painted John the Baptist (p. 46) in an attitude of meditation, next to him a fantastic plant with an apple of Sodom, in a serene landscape, the peace of which is suddenly disturbed by two fantastic structures, marvellous interweavings of dream and reality.

Are these separate paintings or perhaps triptychs of which the other portions have been lost? It is difficult to say. Historical art sleuths have tried to find an answer, sometimes with an imagination worthy of Bosch himself, but the results must always remain inventions as long as one works with parts which are unknown or are merely suppositions.

It is, however, certain that the four panels which are preserved in the Doges' Palace in Venice were once altarpiece wings of a triptych of which the central panel may have represented "The Last Judgment." The four panels show the way to Paradise, Paradise itself, the fall of the damned, and Hell (p. 37). In the Doges' Palace are also to be found "The Triptych with the Hermits," with, on the left, the temptation of St. Anthony, in the centre the penitent St. Jerome (p. 47), and on the right St. Aegidius, and the "Triptych with the Martyrdom of St. Julia."

These pictures show at times some iconographic renovation, but nothing in them gives the slightest hint of the outburst Bosch arrives at in two masterly triptychs: "The Temptation of St. Anthony" (in Lisbon) and "The Garden of Earthly Delights" (in Madrid). It is as though suddenly a veil has been torn open and scenes are disclosed to us which no one could possibly have imagined. All the troubled thought of the late Middle Ages breaks loose, vertiginous and oppressive, a damnation of the whole of human life and of all nature, ferocious satanic dreams to which there seems no end.

Truly a witches' sabbath is the centre panel of "The Temptation of St. Anthony" (p. 38), in which the harassed saint does occupy a central place, but is outnumbered by his demoniacal tormentors. St. Anthony lies kneeling across a little wall of the remains of an abandoned fort in Egypt, in which Jesus can be seen standing, pointing to the crucifix (p. 41). The saint raises two fingers of his right hand to give the sign of the cross. Round him, the world consists of demons, who do not directly lay snares for him, but symbolize evil, which is being committed independently of him and of Christ: simulated charity, lust, dipsomania, deception, pugnacity, and drunkenness. All this is pictured in the most marvellous figures, a never-ceasing stream of hallucinatory apparitions. In the background a city is going up in flames and monsters fly in the air.

On the left-hand panel (p. 39) we see the flying monsters once more, now taking St. Anthony with them in their hellish flight (p. 42). In the foreground he is being carried back to his cave by his companions, who had come upon him apparently dead (p. 40). In the right-hand panel the holy man is sitting on a stone, reading and meditating, surrounded by exhibitions of licentiousness and gluttony (p. 43).

Bosch did not always compose his complicated scenes at once and without later alteration, as he had done in other paintings. Often he would draw them first on the white background of the panels, as, for instance, appears to be the case with the right wing, where the underlying first design is still visible as well as numerous improvements. The composition has been built up organically, and Bosch has attained in this picture, as never before, a precious transparency of colours. "Consummate refinement" are the words to describe the manner in which a grandiose and moving colouration has been constructed with small brushstrokes.

There is refinement too in the sober grisaille painting of the outside of the wings with scenes from the Passion of Christ. One has to imagine the altarpiece closed, with, on the left, Christ being taken prisoner, on the right the Bearing of the Cross, simple and forthright works of art which carry one away through their action. Then the side panels open, and a rich play of colours unfolds itself, sharply contrasting with the grey of the outside—one could almost say that it has the effect of a display of fireworks.

In spite of their sober colours, the outsides of the side panels are none the less interesting. Here Bosch has grimly delineated the scenes of the Passion, in a more genre-like manner similar to that of the early work on the inside, but also more "human-demon-like" and with a rare power of expression in the completed drawing (pp. 44, 45).

The third great triptych is "The Garden of Earthly Delights," the most astonishing of all the works of Bosch. As far as the composition in the centre panel is concerned, this suffers from being too overloaded, and is therefore inferior to "The Temptation of St. Anthony," but, on the other hand, he expresses himself in this work with the greatest clarity and completeness. This painting is like a poem, a work in which Bosch achieves his most authoritative and most subtle power of expression.

Whoever sees in "The Garden of Earthly Delights" a "refined, but monstrously libidinous Freudian dream" is making a terrible mistake. Has ever a painter depicted Paradise in so paradisiacal a manner as Bosch has in this picture? It starts with the left-hand panel, the Earthly Paradise, the Garden of Eden. God holds Eve by the hand and presents her to the amazed Adam. Nothing indicates that these first human beings will one day be driven away from the Garden. Peace reigns, except among the beasts—a lion has struck down a deer or an antelope, a wild boar is fighting with a lizard-like animal, a kind of small panther has a mole in his mouth, but they scarcely disturb the tranquillity of the scene (pp. 62, 64, 65). The marvellous little structures in the background continue in the centre panel (p. 58), which is justly described as "The Garden of Earthly Delights." It has been generally assumed that here man indulges to the full in the carnal lusts which lead him to Hell (in the right-hand panel). This assumption is, however, difficult to maintain if one takes into account the poetry with which Bosch has rendered this "evil." Rather should it be said that the Paradise of the left-hand panel continues in the centre panel, for there is scarcely any criticism from the painter to be perceived regarding the unashamed nudism, or the love play, which is shown in so many variations. Peace prevails everywhere, blacks mingle with whites, men and women stroll about, eat fruits, make love, and bathe in surroundings of supreme bliss (pp, 56, 57, 59). Occasionally the artist hints at the frailty of earthly happiness, such as the lovers who find themselves in a glass ball, or in a strange kind of vessel, or under a glass bell. In the middle portion a continuous rejoicing is expressed by the playful riding of men on partly strange, partly legendary beasts around a pool in which women are bathing (p. 59).

Must we really see in this panel the delirious journey of man to his damnation, as most people suppose? The vanity of earthly life and earthly love? This is difficult to accept, in spite of interpretations of symbolic images. If Hieronymus Bosch had wanted to represent lust, he would have done it much more grimly and much more satirically, as he did in "The Hay Wagon." His nudes here, however, have nothing of passion or of depravity. They seem unaware of their nakedness, for the artist has painted them, almost abstractly, as innocent subjects. Here, then, we are confronted with one of the greatest of the riddles of Bosch, namely: how could this work—and this goes too for "The Hay Wagon" and "The Temptation of St. Anthony"—find a place in the ecclesiastical community? Can it be imagined that the Church authorities accepted these pictures, with their undisguised criticism of the behaviour of monks and nuns, who are shown in all sorts of infamous situations, and with the public exhibition of earthly delights?

81

The answer must surely be in the negative, for we must not forget that these triptychs were painted at a time when attacks on the Church were constantly becoming stronger, and finally led to a revolt—the Reformation. In his book *Das Tausend-jährige Reich* (The Kingdom of a Thousand Years), Wilhelm Fraenger has tried to find an answer by making Bosch a member of one of the heretical sects, the Brothers and Sisters of the Free Spirit, and also of the Homines Intelligentiae, who, among other things, practised nudism, contravened the laws of monogamy, did not fast or go to confession, and as a result were persecuted by the Inquisition.

According to Fraenger, the triptych "The Garden of Earthly Delights" was destined to be used during the sect's services of worship, and in that case the centre panel would not be an attack on voluptuousness, but a glorification of free intercourse between the sexes, by which means the innocence of Paradise could be achieved here on earth.

We have to agree with Fraenger that the current interpretation of the centre panel as depicting the voluptuousness of love as the path to Hell can hardly be justified. It is true that many elements are to be met with which may be taken as symbols of unchastity and sexual passion (birds, fruits, fish, etc.), but the atmosphere of the picture does not by any means indicate this interpretation. Peace and innocence prevail, and that indeed is characteristic of Paradise.

Again, those who think that the right-hand panel could give the solution to all difficulties by an answer to the question of who actually do go to Hell, are also mistaken. Fraenger asserts that it was the followers of the Catholic faith, and, in addition, those people who abandon themselves to worldly pleasures, such as musicians, conjurers, gamblers, and knights. His explanation of the picture of Hell is, however, not compelling enough, and on countless occasions he argues back to the point from which he started.

The riddle of Hieronymus Bosch still remains unsolved, and time and again there are authors who feel themselves called upon to find its solution. Search is made in out-of-the-way corners of religious life. The one classifies Bosch with the Homines Intelligentiae, the other with the Rosicrucians, but proofs to the contrary are always being tendered, and accepted, and ultimately the paintings are buried under so many explanations and interpretations that the work of art itself tends to be forgotten.

Moreover, how can the works of his last period be explained on the basis of the hypothesis that Bosch must have been a member of one or the other persecuted esoteric sect? After the outbursts of fantasy in the great triptychs, it seems as though a sort of lull took place in the work of the artist. Not quite immediately, for first there came the grim pictures of the life of Christ, "The Crowning with Thorns" (p. 66) and "The Bearing of the Cross" (p. 67), if indeed we can agree that these works were executed after "The Garden of Earthly Delights." One might well be inclined to classify them among his earlier work, after "Ecce Homo" (p. 22), for example. The difference in the skill of the artist is, however, so considerable, that the paintings will have to be classified in the last period of Bosch's career.

The realism of both paintings is such that the wickedness of man is presented many times larger than life; in fact, as a caricature. This is particularly the case in "The Crowning with Thorns" (p. 66), where man has become demon, fierce and venomous.

And after all this come the serene works. It seems as though all the devils and all the madness have been driven out of the world. Not a living soul would dare to connect these paintings in any way with heretical sects. Tranquillity now reigns supreme, and at the end of his life Hieronymus Bosch comes to new greatness. For he now produces "The Adoration of the Magi" (p. 69), "The Vagabond," also called "The Prodigal Son" (p. 71), and another "Temptation of St. Anthony" (p. 72), masterpieces of an artist who has ripened and has finally achieved complete peace of mind.

The colouring of "The Adoration" still remains rich, but that of the other two pictures is sober: greys and grey-yellow in "The Vagabond"; quiet browns, greens, and blues in "The Temptation." One feels that Bosch has sacrificed all his former gleaming and brilliant colouration, in order wholly to concentrate upon the spiritual content; upon the representation of the ragged human being who, with timid glance, trudges along his weary way; and upon Saint Anthony, who is sunk in meditation, undisturbed by the insignificant hellish scum surrounding him.

In the serenity and spiritual grandeur of the saint, this "Temptation of St. Anthony" has achieved just as great a perfection as in its colouristic and compositional harmony. Yet the power of this painting is even exceeded by that of "The Vagabond," which is a synthesis of all the talents of Hieronymus Bosch. Since the beginning of our century, as the result of an interpretation by Gluck, this picture has been called "The Prodigal Son." In the past few decades, however, other interpretations have been put forward in which emphasis has been placed on a vagrant, because in the picture too many of the elements deviate from the Biblical parable. In my own opinion the one does not entirely exclude the other, despite astrological interpretations, according to which the vagrant is a Saturn-subject, and as such is bowed down by the grief the planet has caused to our Earth.

Naturally it is very interesting to be aware of the significance of every detail in the picture: of the ladle and the catskin on the basket on the vagrant's back, of the dilapidated tavern with the couple making love in the doorway, of the doves on the roof, of the woman with a mirror behind the window, even of the round shape of the picture itself as a symbol of our globe; but these are all factors of secondary importance. The painting itself, as a work of art, is all the better appreciated when viewed without analysis. From the perfect balance of the composition, the masterly assurance of the brushwork, and the liveliness and expressiveness of the work, one can realize the greatness of the painting, which depicts a wandering man. One has only to look at the vagabond on the outside shutter of "The Hay Wagon" (p. 28) to realize what a complete mastery Hieronymus Bosch had achieved by the end of his life.

We have learned to know Bosch as the most original spirit of the end of the fifteenth century, as a painter whose fantasy has never been equalled by anyone, as a genre painter long before genre painting can be spoken of. One last facet must now be brought to the fore: Hieronymus Bosch as a painter of landscape, for here also he was a renaissant and a pioneer.

It is remarkable how Bosch, in contrast with the demoniacal or grotesque happenings in his foregrounds—and yet somehow in complete unity with them—puts into the backgrounds of most of his paintings complete and actual landscapes, which, it is true, he sees with a poetic eye, but which, for all that, are very real. They are unprejudiced and pure presentations of nature (the Schelde landscape in "St. John at Patmos," p. 55; the landscape in "St. Jerome in Prayer," p. 34; and the Jerusalem-like landscape in "The Adoration of the Magi," p. 68). As the events in his foregrounds become simplified, the landscape occupies a progressively larger place in the picture. The high horizon, necessary in order to have as much space as possible in which to depict the events, becomes lower, and so more and more room becomes available for the landscape as an independent factor (see "The Vagabond," p. 71, and "The Temptation of St. Anthony," p. 72). Not one of his contemporaries regarded the landscape in so progressive a manner as did Hieronymus Bosch. We may come to the conclusion that Bosch looked upon the landscape in the light of its being almost emancipated from the religious painting, a harbinger of the art of Pieter Brueghel the Elder, who in the second half of the sixteenth century was to give landscape a significance of its own.

LIST OF ILLUSTRATIONS

33 THE SHIP OF FOOLS
Panel; 22 × 12⅝ in.; Louvre, Paris

34 ST. JEROME IN PRAYER
Detail with landscape

35 ST. JEROME IN PRAYER
Panel; 31⅞ × 24 in.; Museum of Fine Arts, Ghent

36 ST. CHRISTOPHER
Panel; 44½ × 28⅜ in.; Boymans-van Beuningen Museum, Rotterdam

37 THE WAY TO PARADISE AND HELL
Two panels of an altarpiece; each panel 34 × 15½ in.; Doges' Palace, Venice

38 THE TEMPTATION OF ST. ANTHONY
Central panel; 51¾ × 46⅞ in.; National Museum of Antique Art, Lisbon

39 THE TEMPTATION OF ST. ANTHONY
Left and right panels; each 51¾ × 20⅞ in.

40 THE TEMPTATION OF ST. ANTHONY
Detail from left-hand panel: Two monks and a burgher (supposed self-portrait of Bosch) carry the saint, whom they have found lying as if dead, back to his cave, which has been changed by the Devil into a house of prostitution.

41 THE TEMPTATION OF ST. ANTHONY
Detail from central panel: St. Anthony, kneeling at a low wall, turns round and gives a gesture of blessing. Next to him a noblewoman is offering a plate of soup to a beggar woman, at whose side a man consisting solely of legs and head (supposed self-portrait of Bosch) is sitting. In the background Christ is pointing to a crucifix. Scenes from the Old Testament are on the tower.

42 THE TEMPTATION OF ST. ANTHONY
Detail from left-hand panel: The saint is being carried through the air by demons.